SOUTHEAST ASIAN
CULTURAL HERITAGE

Images of Traditional Communities

The **Institute of Southeast Asian Studies** was established as an autonomous organization in May 1968. It is a regional research centre for scholars and other specialists concerned with modern Southeast Asia, particularly the multi-faceted problems of stability and security, economic development, and political and social change.

The Institute is governed by a twenty-two-member Board of Trustees comprising nominees from the Singapore Government, the National University of Singapore, the various Chambers of Commerce, and professional and civic organizations. A ten-man Executive Committee oversees day-to-day operations; it is chaired by the Director, the Institute's chief academic and administrative officer.

The Programme on the Cultural Heritage of Southeast Asia (CULHERSEA) was established in the Institute of Southeast Asian Studies in 1985 to complement its work on politics, economics, and social change.

Additionally, CULHERSEA plans to build up an extensive archive of photographs, slides, films, and audio cassettes encompassing the wide range of Southeast Asian cultures and traditions. This would be done through a variety of ways, including encouraging individuals to deposit original collections with the Programme. These materials in time should become a valuable resource for research on the cultural heritage of Southeast Asia.

SOUTHEAST ASIAN CULTURAL HERITAGE

Images of Traditional Communities

Compiled by
Ong Choo Suat

Programme on the Cultural Heritage of Southeast Asia
INSTITUTE OF SOUTHEAST ASIAN STUDIES

Published by
Institute of Southeast Asian Studies
Heng Mui Keng Terrace
Pasir Panjang
Singapore 0511

The responsibility for facts and opinions expressed in this publication rests exclusively with the compiler and her interpretations do not necessarily reflect the views or the policy of the Institute or its supporters.

Cataloguing in Publication Data

Ong, Choo Suat
    Southeast Asian cultural heritage: images of traditional communities.
    1. Ethnology — Asia, Southeastern — Pictorial works.
    2. Asia, Southeastern — Social life and customs — Pictorial works.
    I. Pelzer, Dorothy.
    II. Institute of Southeast Asian Studies.
    III. Title.
    DS509.5 059   1986

ISBN 9971-988-33-X

Designed by Chew Kheng Chuan
Typeset by WORDMAKER Design & Typesetting Services
Printed in Singapore by KIM HUP LEE PRINTING CO PTE LTD

Contents

Foreword

Established in 1968, the Institute of Southeast Asian Studies (ISEAS) is an autonomous, regional research centre for scholars and other specialists interested in modern Southeast Asia, particularly its multi-faceted problems of economic development, and political and social change.

To complement its work in politics, economics and social change, the Institute in July 1981 launched a programme of cultural studies, known as the Southeast Asian Cultural Research Programme or SEACURP. It was the Institute's hope that SEACURP would serve as a catalyst to create a greater awareness amongst the Southeast Asian professional and scholarly community — and particularly among the planners and other decision-makers — of the region's cultural heritage and traditions, in terms of the need to evolve more holistic and effective strategies for national and regional development, that is, strategies which could build upon and carry forward the accumulated experiences and cultural heritage of the area into the future. In short, it is hoped that SEACURP might encourage such individuals to view the cultural heritage of the region, and that of particular nations, as an invaluable asset to be utilized and integrated into the making of a richer present and a more fruitful future.

It was also the feeling that SEACURP might be a means to collect resource materials pertaining to Southeast Asian cultures and traditions, with the aim of making these available, through an effective distribution system, to all interested. In this context, an excellent beginning was already assured in that the invaluable collection of slides, photographs, and notes assembled by the American architect, the late Dorothy Pelzer, was available to SEACURP for research at the Institute. It is envisaged therefore that this excellent beginning should in time lead to a larger and varied collection of associated materials pertaining to Southeast Asian cultural traditions and foundations, and to the development of a network of Southeast Asian scholars and professionals — initially comprising those interested in a particular field, for instance, traditional architecture, but eventually involving a group with broader cultural interests cutting across national, sectorial, and disciplinary boundaries.

We are happy to report that SEACURP's efforts over the years have brought a new dimension to the ISEAS Library's collection and services and provided the impetus to improve its ethnographic documentation, leading eventually to the development of an over-arching Programme on the Cultural Heritage of Southeast Asia. This programme will allow for the co-ordination and bringing together of the work and activities of the different groups and individuals engaged in the study of various aspects of the region's cultures, world-views, and traditions, thereby providing for the necessary economies of scale and the potential for effective consolidation of gains made in different segments and at different stages of growth.

Such a programme, apart from its own intrinsic merits and attractions, would be a valuable asset to economists, political scientists, sociologists, and others interested in the contemporary problems of Southeast Asia, as decision-making processes and interpersonal relations cannot be divorced from, or fully comprehended, without a feel for or a proper understanding of the cultural mores and traditions of the different peoples of the region.

We are thus all the more obligated to the various contributors to the Cultural Heritage collection of the Institute, especially Datuk Lim Chong Keat, Project Director of the SEACURP programme, and look forward to their continuing support. In the meantime a modest effort is made here to present a sample of the types of materials already available in the ISEAS Library, in the hope not only that this would be a guide to the nature of the photographs, tapes and other similar research resource materials available, but also that it might stimulate further augmentation of these materials and the research vistas they promise. To facilitate this process, the Library has a scheme by which it provides contributors to the Cultural Heritage collection, with rolls of unexposed films, as well as a duplicate set of the materials deposited. The arrangement will take into consideration the necessity to balance the need to protect the rights of the depositors and the research requirements of scholars using the materials.

In closing we would like to thank all those who have assisted in innumerable ways in making this publication possible. Indeed, it was the late Dorothy Pelzer, architect, photographer, and intrepid traveller, whose collection inspired the development of the Cultural Heritage Programme of the Institute, and the folio that follows is but a humble tribute to her contribution to the study of Southeast Asian cultures.

Kernial S. Sandhu
Director
Institute of Southeast Asian Studies
January 1986

Preface

This folio of photographs features some of the visual materials deposited at the ISEAS Library. Their collectors have assembled the materials to fulfil widely divergent needs. While this has resulted in a rich and vast store of information, it has also created problems in terms of organising the presentation of visual materials for this folio. As it can be a disconcerting exercise to distil 300 visuals from an archive of nearly 70,000 visuals, it will be useful to clarify two points.

First, the visual materials have been presented in two sections: *People in Houses* and *Images of Everyday Life*. The first section features photographs taken by the late Dorothy Pelzer while the second section features photographs from twenty-eight other contributors. Since the materials were collected over a period of nearly forty years, dates are important for placing a photograph in a context, especially when it documents what is no longer there. However, as a proliferation of dates is distracting, the dates have been left unstated in most cases. It is sufficient to note that Dorothy Pelzer took her photographs between 1962 and 1970. A few of the photographs in the second section were taken in the early 1950s. However, unless otherwise stated, the majority of them were taken between 1980 and 1985. Researchers who need information on specific dates will find more details in the list of contributors.

Secondly, both Dorothy Pelzer and the anthropologists among the other contributors often documented the same ethnic groups. Hence, it may be baffling to see photographs of the same ethnic groups appearing in both sections. The Dorothy Pelzer photographs are selected to fit into the theme *People in Houses*, based on a loose geographical grouping. The photographs from the other contributors are selected to fit into themes depicting *Everyday Life*. The thematic arrangement is again flexible as several photographs can be fitted into more than one theme of the following: believing; rejoicing; cooking and eating; planting and harvesting; buying and selling; travelling and resting; working and playing; decorating; healing; remembering.

The overlap is not a result of a paucity of visual materials but rather an indication of the wealth of Southeast Asia's cultural heritage. The same ethnic group presents different research potentials. In this respect, the photographic archive points the way to exciting possibilities for future research development.

Ong Choo Suat

Contributors

The following is a list of the contributors who have generously deposited their materials in the ISEAS Library's Programme on the Cultural Heritage of Southeast Asia (CULHERSEA). Where they have deposited the materials in the Southeast Asian Cultural Research Programme (SEACURP) now located in the Library, this has been so indicated.

In listing our contributors, the primary aim is to state the reason for each contributor collecting the materials deposited — mainly slides and/or photographs, both colour and black-and-white (B/W), and cassette tapes.

Eriko Aoki received her Master of Arts in cultural anthropology from the University of Tokyo. She was collecting materials for a Ph.D. dissertation at the Department of Cultural Anthropology, University of Tokyo, when she took the colour slides and B/W photographs now deposited at ISEAS. She did her field-work in 1979/81, 1982/83 and 1984, researching the oral traditions and rituals of agriculture and the life cycle of three groups of people in central Flores, Indonesia: the Ngadanese, the Endenese and the Lionese.

Fiona Clare lived in Medan for three years in the late 1970s and early 1980s. Out of personal interest, she documented the Bataks of Sumatra and other Indonesians, including the Toraja people and the boat-builders of Sulawesi. She has deposited a selection of colour slides of these people with ISEAS. She lived in Singapore briefly when her husband was posted there and returned to the United Kingdom in 1984.

Wolfgang Clauss collected colour photographs on traditional house-forms in the area of Banda Aceh in 1984 at the request of SEACURP during his tenure as lecturer in the Social Sciences Research Training Centre of Syiah Kuala University, Banda Aceh, Sumatra. He is a lecturer in the Sociology of Development Research Centre, Faculty of Sociology, University of Bielefeld, West Germany. He obtained his Ph.D. in sociology in 1982 from the University of Bielefeld which has published his dissertation on *Economic and Social Change among the Simalungun Batak of North Sumatra.*

Robert B. Cribb collected colour slides and other visual materials on the indigenous built forms of Indonesia in 1983 at the request of SEACURP. He was then conducting field-work on the history of Jakarta during the Indonesian revolution (1945-1949) for which he obtained his Ph.D. in 1984 from the School of Oriental and African Studies, University of London. He is a lecturer in the School of Modern Asian Studies, Griffith University, Australia.

Jacques Dournes is a senior research fellow at the National Centre of Scientific Research, Paris. He obtained his degree in classical studies before he did field-work, principally in the Indochina area between 1946 and 1970 and also in Malaysia and Indonesia. He is known mainly for his publications on the societies of the central Vietnamese highlands. His slides deposited with SEACURP documented several of these societies between 1950 and 1970. He has 185 publications under his name, the major ones including *Forêt femme folie: une traversée de L'imaginaire Jörai; Pötao: une théorie du pouvoir chez les Indochinois Jörai; Akhan: contes oraux de la Forêt indochinoise* and *Mythes Sré: trois pièces de littérature orale d'une ethnie austro-asiatique.*

Gregory L. Forth is an anthropologist whose research interests are the people of eastern Sumba and the Nage people of central Flores, Indonesia. His colour slides and photographs were collected in the course of field-work in eastern Sumba in 1975/76, for which he obtained his Ph.D. from the University of Oxford, and subsequently in central Flores in 1983/84/85. He was until recently the assistant director of the British Institute in South-East Asia, Bangkok. His visuals of eastern Sumba have appeared in his book *Rindi: an Ethnographic Study of a Traditional Domain in Eastern Sumba*.

David E. Hughes researched Indonesian prahu shipping for his Ph.D. dissertation for the Department of Maritime Studies, University of Wales, on "The Indonesian Cargo Sailing Vessels and the Problem of Technology Choice for Sea Transport in a Developing Country". He took his colour slides of traditional sailing boats or prahu in 1980/81 during his field-work in Indonesia and obtained his Ph.D. in 1984. He is now with the Department of Maritime Studies, University of Wales.

Institute for Southern Thai Studies, Srinakharinwirot University, Songkhla, in a joint project with ISEAS, documented in B/W photographs the traditional built form and way of life of villagers in seven provinces of south Thailand in 1985. The Institute is a centre for the study of southern Thai culture and languages, with a strong representation of material culture in its museum. Its archives and library hold an extensive collection of manuscripts, slides, video tapes and cassette recordings.

Khoo Joo Ee is curator of the Museum of the Arts of Asia, Culture Centre, University of Malaya, Kuala Lumpur. She obtained her Ph.D. in art history and archaeology from the School of Oriental and African Studies, University of London. While being trained as an art historian and archaeologist, she developed an interest in ethnographic interpretations of art and archaeological materials. Her Ph.D. dissertation examined the elements from China in Javanese culture during the Majapahit period. Her B/W slides deposited with SEACURP are focussed on these built form.

Victor T. King is a lecturer in the Centre for South-East Asian Studies and the Department of Sociology and Anthropology, University of Hull from which he obtained his Ph.D. in 1981, researching the Maloh of west Kalimantan. This has become one of his major publications: *The Maloh of West Kalimantan: an Ethnographic Study of Social Inequality and Social Change among an Indonesian People*. His colour slides documented the culture of the Maloh in 1972/73 and the Bidayuh and Iban of Sarawak in 1984, during his field trips to Borneo.

Lim Chong Keat is an architect and urban planner in private practice. He obtained his Master of Architecture from the Massachusetts Institute of Technology. He has been Project Director of the Southeast Asian Cultural Research Programme (SEACURP) at ISEAS since its inception in 1981. His interests include historical conservation and the colour slides he deposited with SEACURP are focussed on the traditional culture and built form of Southeast Asia. He is currently working on a photographic exhibition as well as a book on the traditional habitat of Southeast Asia.

Francisco Mañosa is an architect in private practice. He obtained his architecture degree from the University of Santo Tomas, Philippines. His writings and architectural works reflect his interest in the indigenous traditions of his country and his concern for heritage conservation. His colour slides deposited with SEACURP documented mainly the Sulu culture and built form.

Cecilia Ng Siew Hua is currently completing her Ph.D. dissertation at the Department of Prehistory and Anthropology,

School of General Studies, Australian National University. She is researching the material culture of the Minangkabau of Sumatra, Indonesia, focussing on textiles and costumes, their symbolic uses in kinship relationship. Her colour slides and B/W photographs documented these costumes during her field trip there in 1980/81.

Preecha Noonsuk is a lecturer at the Nakon Si Thamarat Teachers College and Secretary of its Centre for the Cultural Studies of Southern Thailand. The Centre has an archaeological and ethnographical museum and an extensive collection of Thai manuscripts. His colour photographs documented the traditional built form of the surrounding area and were taken as part of the Centre's interest in documenting southern Thai culture.

Ong Choo Suat was attached to the Southeast Asian Cultural Research Programme as research assistant to the Project Director between 1981 and 1984. Her slides deposited in SEACURP were collected as a result of fieldwork in Thailand and Malaysia. She is a writer and research worker with an interest in the traditional communities of Southeast Asia.

Ivan Polunin was an associate professor in the Department of Social Medicine and Public Health, Faculty of Medicine, National University of Singapore, prior to his retirement in 1984. He has written substantially on tribal populations and diseases as well as produced a large body of documentaries (writing, sound recording, and filming) on the cultures of Southeast Asia in the 1950s and 1960s, especially for the British Broadcasting Corporation. He currently travels extensively in the course of medical consultancies. His interests include medical anthropology and traditional medicine. His colour slides and B/W photographs taken over the last twenty-five years, documented a wide range of subjects on Southeast Asia.

Ananda Rajah is a research associate at ISEAS and is completing his Ph.D. dissertation for the Department of Anthropology, Research School of Pacific Studies, Australian National University, researching the culture of the Skaw Karen of a village near Chiangmai, north Thailand, with particular reference to their subsistence economy. His colour slides and B/W photographs were taken during his field trip there in 1980/81.

Sharon Siddique and **Nirmala Puru Shotam** are sociologists. Sharon Siddique, a senior fellow at ISEAS, obtained her Ph.D. in sociology from the University of Bielefeld and Nirmala Puru Shotam is currently completing her Ph.D. dissertation at the Department of Sociology, National University of Singapore. The colour slides and cassette tapes they deposited with ISEAS documented the Serangoon Road area in 1981/83, in a study which is part of a larger research project on socio-religious change in the Indian community in Singapore. The materials have appeared in their book *Singapore's Little India: Past, Present and Future.*

Margaret Sullivan is a writer, researcher and artist. During her affiliation as visiting fellow at ISEAS, she collected materials for her research into the cottage industries of Singapore in 1981/84. She has deposited cassette tapes, colour slides and B/W photographs with ISEAS (see Henry Wong and Michael Neo). The materials have been used for her book *"Can Survive La!": Cottage Industries in High-rise Singapore.*

Sumet Jumsai is an architect in private practice. He obtained his Ph.D. from the University of Cambridge. Over the last 20 years, he has been collecting materials in the interest of his practice and concern for the traditional culture and built form of Thailand. He has written on and has initiated numerous projects for historical conservation. His major research work traces the Southeast Asian, Japanese, part of the Chinese and Indian cultures to a common origin in the equatorial West Pacific. This work was first published in Thai in 1982 under the title *NAGA: Oceanic Origins of Culture in the West Pacific and Siam.* It is being translated into English from Thai. His colour slides deposited with SEACURP documented the traditional built form of Thailand and Nias, Indonesia.

Suvit Rungvisai is an associate professor in the Department of Sociology and Anthropology, Faculty of Social Sciences, University of Chiangmai. He has been trained as a lawyer as well as a sociologist and holds degrees in law, political science and sociology. He has written extensively on the issues of politics and nationalism, with particular reference to Thailand, as well as on alcoholism and drug abuse. His colour slides, taken in 1985 at the request of ISEAS, documented the Meo and Karen people of villages in north Thailand.

Tin Maung Maung Than is a research fellow at the Institute of Southeast Asian Studies. He obtained his master's degree in physics from Rangoon University and his Diploma in Economic Planning from the Institute of Economics, Rangoon. His colour slides, taken in 1985, documented the religious and cultural dimensions of social change in Burma. He is currently researching the religion, state and society of contemporary Burma.

Carl A. Trocki is associate professor of history at Thomas More College in Crestview Hills, Kentucky. He obtained his Ph.D. in Southeast Asian history from Cornell University. His research interests include the history of the Malay world in the 18th and 19th centuries as well as the history of Singapore. He is author of *Prince of Pirates: the Temenggongs and the Development of Johor and Singapore, 1784-1885.* He is currently researching the opium trade and opium revenue farms in 19th century Southeast Asia for his

forthcoming book *Opium and the Colonial Economy of Singapore, 1820-1910.* His colour slides taken in 1985, deposited with ISEAS, documented the graves of Malay royalty in Riau, Indonesia, and Chinese rituals in Johor, Malaysia.

Askandar Unglehrt is a lecturer at Universiti Sains Malaysia (USM), teaching the French and German languages. He obtained his Ph.D. from Sorbonne University, Paris. His colour slides deposited with SEACURP documented the boat decorations in Kelantan, Malaysia, in 1977. They were taken for an anthropologist friend, Dr. Paul J. Coatalen also of USM who needed the visual materials for his drawings which were published in *The Decorated Boats of Kelantan: an Essay in Symbolism.*

Wilfried Wagner is professor of history at the University of Bremen. He obtained his Ph.D. from the Goethe University, Frankfurt. His colour slides documented the culture of the Mentawai Island, west of Sumatra, between 1974 and 1981, during which period he made trips there. His deep interest reflects his personal attachment to the Mentawai Islands where he was born while his parents were medical missionaries there.

James F. Warren is senior lecturer in Southeast Asian modern history in the School of Human Communication, Murdoch University, Western Australia. He obtained his Ph.D. from the Australian National University. His B/W slides are recopied historical photographs of rickshaw coolies of early 20th century Singapore. They appeared in his book *Rickshaw Coolie: A People's History of Singapore.* Among his major publications are: *The North Borneo Chartered Company's Administration of the Bajau, 1878-1909;* and *The Sulu Zone, 1768-1898: the Dynamics of External Trade, Slavery and Ethnicity in the Transformation of a Southeast Asian Maritime State.*

Vivienne Wee is an anthropologist who is a lecturer at the Department of Sociology, National University of Singapore, from which she obtained her master's degree for her dissertation on "Religion and Ritual among the Chinese of Singapore". She has completed her Ph.D. dissertation for the Australian National University on "Melayu: Hierarchies of Being in Riau". Her colour slides documented the Malay people in the Riau-Lingga Islands, Indonesia, in 1984.

Henry Wong and **Michael Neo** are professional photographers, the former having set up Henry Wong and Associates, Photographers. Their colour slides and B/W photographs documenting crafts people were specifically taken for Margaret Sullivan's book on the cottage industries of Singapore (see Margaret Sullivan).

Dorothy Pelzer at a Toraja rice granary, Sulawesi, Indonesia

People In Houses:
A Tribute to Dorothy Pelzer

Between 1962 and 1970 Dorothy Pelzer documented the traditional architecture of Southeast Asia, collecting materials for a book which she had entitled *Houses Are People*, demonstrating the initimate relationship between a house and the community which created it. Unfortunately, she did not even finish a draft of the book before she died in 1972, except for a sample chapter on the Angkor temple complex written for submission to publishers.

The following selection is compiled from the black-and-white photographs of the Dorothy Pelzer Collection. The title *People in Houses* is an inversion of her title — partly as a tribute to her and mainly because it aims at showing the people side of the house story, as seen through her eyes, in what was essentially rural Southeast Asia during that period.

The concept of the house, as Pelzer realized, extends beyond the dwelling, which the house has come to mean in the contemporary, urban context. The dwelling is an important structure in a community but there are also other important structures. These include the temple, shrine, granary, clan house and boat, depending on the needs of each community, for example, whether it is a riverine or a mountain community. Each structure is valued and put up with rituals and endowed with cosmological significances to ensure the well-being of those who use it.

This selection of photographs features both the house and the people, confirming Pelzer's strong indication of the intimacy existing between them — whether the people actually put up the structure or conceptualized it while craftsmen put it up. This relationship was often complex and one could see that it would not be inappropriate to state that the community created the structure which grew in an organic fashion. Pelzer described this in an undated letter (c. 1963), written as usual, in a hurry to freshly commit ideas to paper, using an informal but expressive style which caught her mood of exhilaration:

> That's the exciting [aspect] about architectural form: it has a life of its own! You can't push it around. It flowers according to the unselfconscious urgencies of life. . .

The unselfconscious urgencies of life provide the incentive for creativity in many instances. A Borneo long-house has a new apartment added to it when a young couple starts a family, and longhouses have been known to grow and grow. The open platform for drying food and clothes can become a covered walkway for shelter from rain and sun and for indoor work.

Other urgencies of life extend the community beyond the house and its environs, as Pelzer carefully recorded. Her documentation included people working in the fields, in the markets, in the temples and participating in community activities such as weddings, funerals and religious ceremonies.

On the one hand, it is reassuring to know that Pelzer's documentation includes scenes which still exist today although her earliest photographs date back twenty years. Scenes include people chatting on open platforms, at doorways, and in open-air markets, women weaving underneath houses on stilts, wizened old people crafting and so on. As a result of this, Pelzer's images give us a sense of continuity which transcend the passage of time.

However, changes and continuities exist side by side. Changes include the winning of independence from colonial powers, political upheavals, urbanization and modernization, and the resulting confusion from having to give up many traditional practices.

The urban centres have been drastically transformed and urbanization is an unyielding tide creeping across the countryside. House-forms are among the first to be affected: corrugated iron replaces the thatch roof, often as a sign of wealth and prestige while plywood panels are convenient replacements when richly carved wooden ones rot or are sold to tourists.

The value of the Dorothy Pelzer Collection is therefore twofold: the photographs confirm what existed at that time. Where changes have taken place, her record of the past is priceless. This is especially so with regard to house-forms, as many of those she documented no longer stand. Where they still stand, her record is a good measure of the state they were in.

Those who have used the collection — both the researcher and the casual visitor — find the visuals stunning. Her photographic skill was evident and her response to her subject, especially people, was sensitive. Researchers, mainly architects and anthropologists, have benefitted, each deriving a different set of information for his particular area of interest.

The black-and-white photographs in this selection have been loosely collated on a geographical basis, although cultural affinities cut across national boundaries at times. For example, many culture groups can be found on both the Kalimantan (Indonesian) and the Malaysian segments of Borneo island. A similar situation exists among the hill-tribe people of Burma, Thailand, Laos and Cambodia.

Compiling the text to this selection has been both challenging and frustrating. From the information contained in the Dorothy Pelzer Collection, it was possible to obtain an outline of Pelzer's educational background and professional experiences before she went to Southeast Asia in 1962. After 1962, her letters to friends and specialists are the best available sources of information. However, very little is known of her personal life except that she was divorced by the time she started on her research and that she was a Christian Scientist. According to a cousin, Pelzer obtained her pilot's license during her university years in Cornell. This rare achievement for a woman living in the 1930s is an early indication of her adventurous and pioneering spirit.

Pelzer left very little formal writing among her notes and papers. Noteworthy exceptions are her sample chapter on the Angkor temple complex and her two manuscripts: "Footpath to Shangri-La", describing her travels in Nepal in 1959; and "Trek Across Indonesia", describing her travels in Indonesia in 1965, which was published posthumously (Singapore: Graham Brash, 1982).

The short biographical note she prepared for publishers and funding agencies reads stiffly and actually masks her warm, vibrant personality. This shows up in her letters and notes, which are often fragmentary, being in incomplete sentences, a clutch of phrases, and half-formed thoughts quickly committed to paper. Nonetheless, they vividly express her moments of ecstacy and despair.

Since 1972, many publications have appeared which have given more space to visuals, ranging from the academic to the journalistic. Still, Pelzer's efforts remain relatively unmatched by any other individual in terms of its extensive coverage, the focus on house-forms and the persistence with which she carried out the ambitious programme she set for herself.

Dorothy Pelzer (1915-72)

Dorothy West Pelzer was born in New Jersey, USA, on 6 May 1915. She studied at Cornell University and later at the Principia College, Elsah, Illinois, where she obtained her B.A. (Hons.) degree in 1937. After teaching for a year at the University of Rochester, New York, she studied at the Institute of Design in Chicago.

The Institute of Design was initially known as the New Bauhaus. The Bauhaus was the most significant school of art in Germany in the 1920s, under Walter Gropius. When political developments led to its closure in the early 1930s, the Bauhaus model for training designers, architects and artists was transplanted to the United States by its founding members, especially Gropius and Laszlo Moholy-Nagy.

Pelzer was at the Institute from 1937 to 1941, where she did sculpture workshop under Moholy-Nagy, weaving, photography and design. Her background interests included the performing arts (dancing and music).

She taught dance and sculpture at the Principia College from 1941 to 1943 before working as an architectural designer at Container Corporation of America in Chicago between 1943 and 1947.

She had begun to think seriously of a career in architecture even when she was at the Institute of Design, as a result of a second-year project, which was the use of sculpture to delineate and enhance architectural space. Photographs of a part of this project appeared in *Vision in Motion* by Moholy-Nagy (Chicago: Paul Theobald, 1947, p. 231).

In 1947, she went to the Massachusetts Institute of Technology (MIT) where she obtained a master's degree in architecture in 1950. At MIT, she was also a teaching fellow in visual fundamentals under Gyorgy Kepes.

Subsequently, Pelzer both practised and taught architecture. She was a staff member of Wellesley College, Massachusetts, from 1954 to 1955, where she gave courses in medieval and modern architecture. She practised architecture till 1958, designing a wide range of buildings, from factories in Chicago to suburban houses in New England.

There was one professional experience which she particularly valued and which was relevant to her research in Southeast Asia: she built a small house with her own hands on her forty-acre property in Conway, New Hampshire, where she was a registered architect. Building one's own house with one's own hands was a skill which many Southeast Asians practised and Pelzer felt that this skill had been lost in contemporary architecture.

She explained this when she was jotting down ideas to write to publishers in 1969:

> After a more or less conventional architectural education . . . I felt the need to experience elementary building techniques for myself and in that way built my own house, working in materials . . . [to make up for] what's being lost in the way of human contact . . . by our technological civilisation — which is in some ways magnificient, in sending man to the moon, but in other ways overwhelms and destroys something in man which is beautiful and necessary . . .

Pelzer's elder sister, Marion Pelzer, wrote this of the small house in Conway:

> Dot has built the house entirely by herself, with the help of friends. Labor costs have not exceeded $17. Dot says that she learned a lot by doing things herself, and the trial and error method has helped her appreciate architectural problems. The weekend I was there she decided to change things, and she tore out the few bits of solid wall, put them in other places, and substituted glass panels.

Pelzer's first contact with Asia was a study tour in 1958-59, when she spent seven months in the rural areas of Japan, documenting traditional house-forms. The remainder of the period was spent in Southeast Asia, India, Nepal and, to a lesser extent, in the Middle East.

This trip made an impact on her and was to change her life. On reflection, when she was preparing to present to publishers her proposal for *Houses Are People*, she wrote:

> I was determined to have a permanent record of the folk/indigenous architecture . . .
> I wanted to record the buildings which most directly and completely express the people themselves . . . from the long-houses of Borneo (showed communal living) to the far overhanging roofs of Toradja —
> . . .
> Virtually nothing has been done before in documenting this subject. Monumental architecture in Asia — the temples and the tomb — is well known. But folk architecture is largely

unknown, except for material recorded here and there in dusty journals by anthropologists, who while recording valuable and pertinent facts about the society rarely see visual or structural form.

. . .

The story on houses is not a little thing. The term "domestic architecture" would imply a differentiation from "religious architecture" or "monumental architecture". But these houses are in many cases inseparable from religious architecture. In many primitive societies the house also includes the temple function. All the houses express the fundamental attitudes of the traditional adat or customary law in social relationships, obligations, and respect for "the spirits" — attitudes which are changing, maybe going under cover, but which have not disappeared in the present time.

Pelzer left for Southeast Asia as an IVS (International Voluntary Service) volunteer in September 1962. IVS was a privately funded USA aid programme which Pelzer was attached to until mid-1963. She was posted to Vientiane, Laos, where she was involved in designing school buildings in Luang Prabang and Pakse. But the design work was not in line with her interest in folk architecture. Soon, she felt the frustration of not working in the villages, making people-to-people contact with the Laotians and not just the officials. She was also mainly desk-bound, partly because of security problems which made it difficult to visit the villages. She wrote to friends that by May 1963 permission had to be obtained two days ahead for travel beyond a six kilometre radius outside Vientiane. This explains the thinness of her materials on Laotian folk architecture.

Before she left IVS, Pelzer was commissioned to design the USA pavilion for the State Fair which was and still is a big religious and social event in Vientiane, held annually in November at the site of the great Buddhist stupa called That Luang. The pavilion was finished in October, by which time Pelzer had left IVS. The structure was constructed from bamboo and she had made it roofless "because it never rains during That Luang". But that year it did rain. Still, her design won the first prize.

She was particularly elated by the reaction of the highest ranking Laotians. She wrote to friends a few months later from Bangkok:

So I had some fun up there with long bamboos and a trench digger, and this year the USA exhibit was full of spatial grace . . . What pleased me most . . . was that General Phoumi, Boun Oum, and the King — according to my sleuths — were heard to marvel: "But this is *Beautiful* — and all with native materials!"

After she left IVS, Pelzer decided to stay on in Southeast Asia, using her own funds for research. By then, she knew that she wanted to document as fast as possible the fine traditional house-forms which were decaying or being destroyed at an alarming rate. Her documentation testifies to the amount of decay or destruction which have since taken place.

She was also distressed by the attitudes of most Southeast Asians especially the professionals — architects and planners. Some professionals were unperturbed by the decay and destruction, which was often taking place without even a record of the house-forms lost. At times they were the agents of change themselves, in using imported materials.

As they were involved in the designing and planning of contemporary urban landscapes, they were in a good position to exercise influence in creating awareness of the traditional elements in architecture. The following quote from one of Pelzer's letters from Bangkok, dated February 1964, sums up the situation:

They're learning from us at such a rate — learning at least the superficialities and forgetting their "own" — that I think we've got to catch what we can of "theirs" — quick! — before it's lost to all of us forever. Not that the old forms should be preserved as a "style" to be imitated in reinforced concrete! But the recognition of what their genius produced in former times should strengthen [their] creativity today. They're awfully good at imitating. Not so good right now at creating — because mainly uncertain of what their values really are.

In this letter, Pelzer had in mind the urban architects and planners. At the same time, in situations where villagers constructed their own house-forms, Pelzer also realized that a similar process of change was taking place. These changes could mean the replacement of the traditional with what might represent "progress". She expressed her fears in *Trek across Indonesia* (p. 2):

> The most interesting of these houses everywhere were fast becoming lost — built as they were in perishable wood, bamboo, and thatch, in a physical climate taking heavy toll of such materials, and in a mental climate fast abandoning old forms in the rush for imported "progress".

For eight years, Pelzer travelled extensively in nine Southeast Asian countries: Burma, Cambodia (Kampuchea), Laos, Thailand, Vietnam, Malaysia, Singapore, Indonesia and the Philippines. She assembled over 38,000 images (31,000 black-and-white negatives and photographs; 7,000 colour slides) and six filing cabinet drawers of notes as well as other materials.

From mid-1969, Pelzer stayed mainly at Ringlet, Cameron Highlands, a Malaysian mountain resort. There, she sifted through her notes, slides and photographs, trying to consolidate what she had collected. She managed to write the sample chapter on the Angkor temple complex, finish a layout schema for *Houses Are People*, and do a preliminary selection of visuals and an outline of her book, but the bulk of the work remained undone. She realized that her strong feelings about taking "that pure first look" was right and that she alone could judge for herself.

In *Trek across Indonesia*, p. 99 she described this during an interview:

> A scholarly Batak came over to talk one morning, and we plunged into philosophy and terminology and symbols. "Of course you have read what Winkler says . . ." I said I hadn't. ". . . and Veerhoeve and Tichelman . . . and Bergama?" I had to confess I hadn't. He looked accusing. What kind of scholarship was this? I had to defend myself. "All of this would have

to come." I said — but later. "It may seem strange to you," I said, "but first I want to look directly. The life and architecture have something to say themselves — without one's knowing too many European interpretations. That pure first look can be had just once. Then I want to ask my own questions — of Indonesians. Later, I can read." This was something unheard of! To look upon life with one's own unscholarly eyes! He smiled benignly.

Pelzer was especially distrustful of scholars who wrote books from research in libraries, without the benefit of field-work, which she felt was such an important part of the exercise. From those who did do field-work, she did use their visual documentation as important source materials. However, she ultimately wanted her book to be "an impetus to creative action and not just another dusty tome". She described this in an undated letter from Ringlet:

> Every photograph gets an analysis right down to its root! And [in] doing so I find out what makes these houses tick. Fortunately, I've found that most of the time I have pointed the camera in the right direction — so that there is an enormous amount of fact — right there for the seeing, if I am patient enough to study and dig for it. And these facts I can trust — whereas things other people have written are often erroneous or mis-seen.

In 1970, Pelzer returned to the USA for six months, trying to see publishers regarding *Houses Are People*. Two major publishing houses offered her contracts which she took back to Ringlet to consider. Unfortunately, she became seriously ill with cancer in 1971. She stayed with friends in Singapore before returning to the United States where she died in April 1972.

For six years, Pelzer financed her own research. In 1968 and 1971, she received grants from the JDR 3rd Fund (John D. Rockefeller), which provided her with much needed financial support as well as a sympathetic appreciation that her work was important. She was particularly grateful to Porter McCray, Director of the JDR 3rd Fund, for his encouragement.

Among her last papers, McCray found that she had designated her Malaysian friend, Lim Chong Keat, as the person who should carry on her research because of his training as an architect and especially because he had discussed with her their mutual concern for the fate of traditional house-forms.

Lim also obtained his master's degree from MIT and is an architect and urban planner in private practice in Singapore and Malaysia. In August 1972, Lim was requested by JDR 3rd Fund to carry on Pelzer's research work. As she did not leave a manuscript for *Houses Are People*, he felt that her approach was so personal that no one, let alone himself, could do justice to her intentions. After careful consideration, in 1978, Lim, McCray, and Richard Lanier (who became Director of the JDR 3rd Fund when McCray retired) decided to set up the Dorothy Pelzer Collection as an archive for research, especially as an impetus to stimulating more Southeast Asian scholarship.

In 1979 and 1980, the JDR 3rd Fund awarded Lim two grants to assemble and organize the materials to make them retrievable. Designated the Pelzer Research Project, the work by Lim and his associates was to collate, inventorize and house the collection — from the task of assembling it from various locations in Ringlet and the United States to housing it in proper storage systems to replace the make-shift storage it was in previously. To conserve funds, Pelzer had used shoe-boxes for her photographs and old envelopes for many of her notes, for instance.

In 1981, the Institute of Southeast Asian Studies (ISEAS) offered host facilities for the collection (office space, administrative back-up and storage facilities, including twenty-four-hour air-conditioning/dehumidification), while the Toyota Foundation provided funding for a three-year programme called Southeast Asian Cultural Research Programme (SEACURP). ISEAS has custody of the collection for the present under the direction of Lim Chong Keat, and the Asian Cultural Council (which superseded the JDR 3rd Fund in 1980) overseas the custodianship.

As Project Director of SEACURP, Lim aims at creating a base whereby Southeast Asian research scholars, with their counterparts elsewhere, can evolve strategies for cultural development.

This aim fits in well with Pelzer's concern that more Southeast Asians should be aware of the value of their disappearing house-forms. To those who are the decision-makers, she only asked that they make their decisions wisely. In a letter to a Laotian friend, written in February 1964, she wrote:

> I do not advocate holding back inevitable change but sometimes we can be guided in the present by an intelligent evaluation of the past.

BURMA

1-4: A Buddhist attiring for the act of making merit, probably in offering food to the monks. He carries a container, called *soon-ok* or *soon-it*, for curry and rice.

5

7

5-6: A *pongyi*'s or monk's funeral in Meiktila. The decorative papier mâché shelter probably indicates a high-ranking monk, whose photograph rests on the catafalque at left.

7: A *shinpyu* ceremony in Mandalay, held for boys and girls entering puberty. Boys become novices for a short period, gaining their parents much merit, while girls have their ears pierced. The elaborate and expensive ceremony enhances their parents' social prestige.

8: A musician at *shinpyu* ceremony.

THAILAND

9: The house of the Bunnag family in Bangkok.

10-11: At a home in Bangkok.

12: A Lao Song house in Phetburi.

13: Building a *kuti*, or monks' quarters, within a temple compound, in Prapadaeng, near Bangkok.

14: Building the same *kuti*.

15-16: River scenes at Uthai.

17

18

17-18: A village near Ban Houei Sai, near Chiangmai in north Thailand.

19: The woman weaving under the house could be a T'ai Lü, a hill people.

19

CAMBODIA

20: River scene at Siem Reap. The water-wheel at left is an irrigation device.

21-22: A woman weeding an onion field and a young girl balancing a water jar. Both of them use a *kramar*, a multi-purpose cloth which can be fashioned as headgear for protection from the sun or as a base for balancing items on the head. Pelzer photographed them at Chroui Dang, near Phnom Penh.

20

21

23

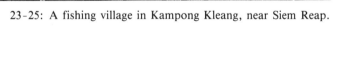

23-25: A fishing village in Kampong Kleang, near Siem Reap.

24

25

26

26-27: Scenes at Kampong Kleang.

27

LAOS

28: An old man making thatch in a village near Luang Prabang.

29: Popcorn vendor in Vientiane.

30

31

32

30-32: A high-ranking Laotian who was president of the Laotian women's association.

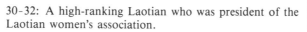

VIETNAM

33-34: The waterfront at Danang. The basket boats are called *thuyền thúng* in the north, and *ghe thúng* in the centre and south of the country.

35: A Chinese Vietnamese courtyard in Saigon, now Ho Chi Minh City.

36–38: Scenes in Hué: the
waterfront and the
market; and the gate at
the Queen Mother's
palace.

37

38

39-40: A Montagnard smoking a pipe by the doorway of her home. The cut log is the staircase to the home, as the man in the second photograph demonstrates. Firewood is stored under the house which has walls made of woven material. The Montagnards are the hill people of the central Vietnamese highlands.

41: Husking padi on an open platform in a Rhade village in Ban Me Thuot. The Rhade are a Montagnard group.

MALAYSIA

42: A Malay house at Kampong Cheng in Malacca.

43: The house of Tun Tan Cheng Lock, a prominent Malaysian leader, in Heeren Street, Malacca, in 1968. The street is now renamed Jalan Tun Tan Cheng Lock after him.

44

44: A Kenyah man in Sarawak working on the verandah of his longhouse.

45: Berawan women preparing food in Sarawak. The woman at right has her arms and feet tattooed.

46: Berawan at a longhouse feast in Sarawak.

47

48

49

47: A Rungus Dusun woman at work inside her longhouse, in Sabah.

48-49: Rungus Dusun woman and man in *adat* clothes. The Rungus Dusun often wear heavy metal ornaments around the neck, arms and legs.

50: Rungus Dusun woman at the door to her longhouse apartment in Sabah.

INDONESIA

51: A wedding in Solo, Java.

52: Musicians at the wedding.

53

54: Scene at the same wedding.

55: Dancers performing for the wedding guests.

56: Performers "riding horses" made from colourfully decorated bamboo in a dance form called *kuda-lumping*, *kuda* meaning "horse". As the dancing approaches the climax, performers are whipped. They go into a trance, and behave like horses and chew grass, for instance. The *kuda-lumping* is a popular form of entertainment for weddings and other festive occasions.

56

57: The market in Rante Pao, Sulawesi.

58

60

59

58-60: Market activities in Rante Pao, Sulawesi. Only the women wear the distinctive hats.

61: A display of family gongs at Desa Elu in Waikabubak, in west Sumba.
Pelzer described Desa Elu as a tiny kampong of only seven to eight houses (*Trek Across Indonesia*, p. 27).

Scenes at Waikabubak, west Sumba.

62: A woman plaiting what looks like a basket.

63: A woman working in front of the village megaliths.

64: An old woman minding the pigs.

65

65: The interior of a house in a village in Pongkor, Flores, showing the cooking area in the background.

66-67: Thatching the roof of a house in Pongkor, Flores.

68: The village centre, Todo, Flores.

69-70: Scenes at Wolo Topo, a village which is an hour and a half's walk from Ende, on the southwest coast of Flores.

71: A Ngada woman holding a bamboo tube in front of the rice granaries in her village. The Ngada people live in south Flores, near the coast around the Inerie volcano, and inland on the high Badjava plateau.

72-74: Elaborate dance ritual at a *gondang* in a Toba Batak village. A *gondang* is held for many possible reasons, including the celebration of weddings, funerals and the rituals of building a new house. On this occasion, the celebration honours an old couple whose coffins have just been completed. The Toba Bataks are the largest of the Batak group of people living in Sumatra.

74

75: An old man at the *gondang* wears an *ulos* round his shoulders. The *ulos* is a traditional shawl which is highly treasured, often as a family heirloom. For instance, it can be used to mark status in society, to signify kinship, to welcome babies into the world and for funerary purposes.

76: At home in Batu Sangkar in west central Sumatra, the traditional homeland of the Minangkabau.

76

77: On the river at Bulak Monga, on the Sikakap Straits which separate North Pagai from South Pagai, the southern islands of the Mentawai chain. The woman wears a palm-leaf skirt and hat, and a tree-bark 'coat' which offer protection from rain and sun during work. This includes fishing, when the women are immersed up to the chest. Both the men and women wear the palm-leaf hats.

78: A youth on the open platform of his home in Bulak Monga.

79

79: The supporting timber of a house in Onohondro in south Nias.

80: The kitchen of an Apayao house. The Apayao are shifting cultivators who live in the far north of Luzon, in an area drained by the Apayao River system.

81: A child at the doorway of a Maranao house in Bacolod Chico, which is located near Lanao del Sur, the largest deep water lake in the southern Philippines.

82: Another Maranao house. This one is made of bamboo and is in Masiu, another location in Lanao del Sur.

83: Guests and musicians arriving by boat for a wedding at Sitankai, which is on the Sibutu group of islands in the extreme south of the Sulu Archipelago.

84: The musicians performing outside the house.

85: The bridal couple with attendants and guests at the wedding at Sitankai.

86

87

86-87: The same wedding party leaving.

TAIWAN

88-89: A Yami village and boats. The Yami people are found solely on Lanyu, an island some 70 kilometres south of Taiwan.

89

88

Images of Everyday Life:
The Role of Visual Documentation

The collections of materials deposited with the Library's Programme on the Cultural Heritage of Southeast Asia and the Southeast Asian Cultural Research Programme form an archive which encompasses a wide range of research areas, disciplines and personal interests. Over the last four years, these two Programmes have built up a substantial archive enriched by contributors who have generously decided that they are willing to share original research materials with others in the interest of scholarship.

There are collections which have been assembled over long periods of twenty to twenty-five years and their contributors have felt that the process of depositing their materials for further research have re-vitalised their efforts when they are re-analysed by new generations of scholars. Others have assembled their collections through the arduous task of preparing for their publications or dissertations.

The archive contains both audio as well as visual materials. The audio section (of cassette tapes) will be developed but it is currently proportionately much smaller than the visual section which consists of slides, photographs, negatives and video tapes/movies, both colour and black-and-white (B/W). The subsequent discussion basically pertains to visuals.

The most important feature of this archive is its availability for further analysis by scholars and interested individuals in similar or related disciplines taking each collection beyond the parameters of its original research boundary. Numerically, the archive holds over 70,000 images, covering a variety of research areas, including architecture, folk art, anthropology, archaeology, traditional medicine and urban sociology.

Qualitatively, it contains a high proportion of images and other materials which are "literate". In most instances, each contributor has a special focus and each visual image frames the information he needs — for recall, as an aid to remembering complementary details, for further analysis when he has time to sit down at a desk, after field-work, and for future use in publications and lectures. Aesthetics do not take priority although there is a good number of visuals constituting good photography.

The information content of an image is the criterion of its value. For this reason, even a blurred image which provides crucial evidence of a rare ceremony, or, for that matter, a poor cassette recording of an interview with an aged person, is very valuable.

The "literacy" of an image also comes with the data a contributor assembles with his materials: date, location, subject matter and the context in which the visual is acquired. Most times, a certain amount of premeditation goes into the collection of materials. The contributor will have studied the situation before going into the field. An anthropologist for instance will not only need to know the time, location and date of a ritual but also the symbolic and cultural significances of what he is documenting. In the case of a rarely performed ritual, in an isolated community, the importance of being able to record the event is in itself an achievement, once one becomes aware of the tragedy of non-achievement in many historical expeditions. Charles Livingstone the official photographer to his brother David's expedition to Zambesi in 1858 was not successful in collecting photographic images.

In its development, the archive is weighted towards certain areas and disciplines. With the setting up of the Programme on the Cultural Heritage of Southeast Asia, there is a good assembly of materials on urban sociology and anthropology, a result of special projects associated with ISEAS and contacts with resource persons using the Library. Furthermore, as a result of the impetus provided by SEACURP's focus on traditional architecture, there is a strong representation of visuals on the built form and house-forms of Southeast Asian cultures, (built form covering a wide range of structures, including boats, non-house structures like shrines, pavilions and field huts).

This weightage has also to be considered against the fact that certain disciplines and areas of research lend themselves to visual and audio documentation more readily than others: architecture, art history and the study of material culture involving concrete images are more effectively documented visually, with annotations forming an important adjunct. A house-form or an art object, for instance, can be more rapidly and effectively documented with a camera than in textual description. Additionally, visuals have an impact which is an aid to recall.

The value of each collection can be assessed and accumulated at four possible levels:

1   Its value to the individual contributor who collected the materials for his specific area of research.

2   Its value to researchers in similar and related areas of research and discipline.

3   Its timeless value as a record, especially documentation of traditions and forms which no longer exist.

4   Its applicability for educational and mass media uses.

The accumulative value of a collection is probably best seen in an examination of the Dorothy Pelzer Collection against the history of documentation in Southeast Asia. When Dorothy Pelzer started her work, whatever visual documentation existing then was known only to the specialists. Thus, Borneo specialists would know Charles Hose who documented the tribes in Sarawak in the late nineteenth century when he was in the service of the Second Rajah Brooke for twenty-four years as an administrator as well as a naturalist and collector of ethnographica. He collaborated with W. McDougall in writing *The Pagan Tribes of Borneo*, 2 volumes (London: Macmillan, 1912).

Similarly, those who researched the mountain people of north Luzon would know Albert Jenks who documented the Bontoc Igorot in 1903 when he was chief of the Ethnological Survey of the Philippines Islands. Jenks was at one time the assistant ethnologist at the Smithsonian Institution in Washington, D.C., and later Chairman of the Department of Anthropology in the University of Minnesota. His research experience culminated in the publication of *The Bontoc Igorot* (Manila: Bureau of Public Printing, 1905).

Firstly, their work provided a baseline for the development of documentation at a time when photography was increasingly recognised as an important tool of research. Their pioneering efforts gave documentalists the basis for development. Thus, Pelzer could compare their images with what she saw fifty to sixty years later.

The Bontoc Igorot, for instance, were then existing in isolation. Access to their domain was a journey of considerable length over rough mountain terrain by foot. By the time Pelzer visited the same area, roads had been built for vehicles and non-indigenous materials were being imported for use in the building of their house-forms.

Secondly, the published works of these documentalists form only a part of their collections, especially in terms of visual materials. These collections, now mainly reposited in museums and archives, are of great value to researchers of many disciplines. Thus Pelzer could research visual documentation of house-forms from collections of materials which are essentially ethnographic in focus. She had the advantage of a survey of materials dating from the late nineteenth century to the late 1930s and her own documentation benefitted considerably from this baseline.

The late 1930s is a feasible cut-off point because the valuable documentation of ethnography was interrupted by World War II and did not start again till the late 1940s and the early 1950s when a new generation of documentalists had the added advantage of improved photographic equipment. A small but significant amount of documentation of cultures went on for military reasons. One example which comes readily to mind is Tom Harrisson who worked with the Kelabits during World War II as part of British intelligence activities in the interior of northern Borneo. His experiences, which included a study of the peoples of that area, were recorded in *The World Within* (London: Cresset Press, 1959).

Pelzer's remarkable contribution to the documentation of architecture and ethnography is her in-depth study of traditional house-forms in a coverage of over thirty cultures in nine Southeast Asian countries. She was the first to have done this, however incomplete her task may seem, and no single individual has since matched her efforts.

The Dorothy Pelzer Collection now forms another baseline for the development of documentation. There have been researchers who have made use of her collection since her death in 1972. For example, Jerome Allen Feldman used her photographs and notes for his Ph. D. dissertation for Columbia University, 1977, on "The Architecture of Nias, Indonesia, with special reference to Bawamataluo Village."

Thus, although it was a handicap that Pelzer herself did not use her materials for publications of her own, her work lives on through the research work of others and her materials will continue to give new directions to future generations.

The collections deposited with the archive have been assembled for basically five reasons (for other details which do not appear here, please see list of Contributors).

1   There are contributors with in-depth focus on a particular culture, collecting materials for their Ph. D. dissertations which they are currently completing or have completed. They are Eriko Aoki, David E. Hughes, Cecilia Ng Siew Hua, Ananda Rajah and Vivienne Wee. All of them are anthropologists except Hughes who researched Indonesian prahu shipping.

2   There are contributors who collected the materials which constitute important documentation for their work. They include researchers such as anthropologists Gregory L. Forth, Victor T. King and Jacques Dournes; sociologists Sharon Siddique and Nirmala Puru Shotam; historians Carl A. Trocki and James F. Warren; art historian Khoo Joo Ee; medical anthropologist Ivan Polunin; economist Tin Maung Maung Than and writer Margaret Sullivan. They also include professional architects Lim Chong Keat, Sumet Jumsai and Francisco Mañosa. In particular, the development of the SEACURP archive is due to the efforts of its Project Director Lim Chong Keat who has travelled extensively and made many field trips to contact resource persons and acquire materials for the collection.

3   There are contributors who have unselfishly taken time off their own research to collect materials at the request of SEACURP and the Library. An acknowledgement of appreciation is recorded here to Wolfgang Clauss, Robert B. Cribb and Suvit Rungvisai.

4   There are contributors who are photographers for books written by others: Askandar Unglehrt, Henry Wong and Michael Neo.

5   There are also contributors whose deep personal inter-

ests give them the impetus to go on collecting materials indefinitely: Fiona Clare on the Indonesian
peoples, including the Bataks of Lake Toba and the
Toraja of Sulawesi and Wilfried Wagner on the Mentawai Islands, west of Sumatra, the place of his birth.

The archive at ISEAS is a specialist archive, at present
composed mainly of in-depth studies of specific cultures.
The images following this essay have been selected and
grouped thematically to give some idea of the richness of
cultural life in this region as well as the breadth of interest of
the contributors. The future growth of the archive will de-
pend to a great extent on the willingness of potential contributors to deposit their materials in the cause of history,
documentation and research. The Programme on the Cultural Heritage of Southeast Asia is designed to provide a
large enough umbrella under which a wide range of interests
can be accommodated. Conditions of deposit provide for the
protection of the legitimate rights of the contributor on the

one hand and the needs of the researcher on the other hand.
The materials are housed under approved environmental
conditions of storage and preservation. In this way, it is
hoped that the Library will be able to develop a research
resource that will supplement and complement its collections in publications, microfilms and other print form. It
is crucial that this archive continues to grow as a custodian
of this region's heritage.

References

1   Cantwell, Ann-Marie, ed. "The Research Potential of
     Anthropological Museum Collections," *Annals of the
     New York Academy of Sciences* (Dec. 1981).

2   Hockings, Paul, ed. *Principles of Visual Anthropo-
     logy*. World Anthropology Series. The Hague:
     Mouton, 1975.

3   Sontag, Susan. *On Photography*. New York: Dell
     Publishing Co., 1977.

BELIEVING

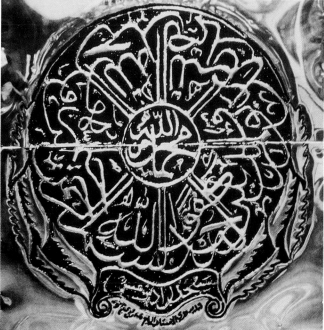

92: A Minangkabau wedding in Sumatra. At this stage, men from the bridegroom's matrilineage and the bridegroom (with tie) are at the bride's home, being ceremonially offered betel nut by women from the bride's lineage.
Cecilia Ng

90-91: Inscriptions from the Holy Quran in embossed metal in a Singapore mosque. The artist stands besides his work which adorns the *mimbar* or pulpit.
Henry Wong and Michael Neo

93: Young girls praying in a curtained area in the Penyengat mosque in Riau, Indonesia. An adult is in attendance.
Vivienne Wee

94: Minangkabau villagers in Sumatra reciting the Quran in a mosque during the fasting month.
Cecilia Ng

93

94

95-97: Expressions of Buddhism and religious belief take many forms in Burma. At the country's holiest shrine, the Shwedagon Pagoda in Rangoon, a reclining Buddha is housed inside a pavilion while a *dvarapala* or guardian spirit (95) stands outside another pavilion on the main platform. A woman offers a shawl (96) to the *Nan-Karaing Lady of Pegu*, the guardian spirit of the district at the shrine near the top of the Hinthagon Hill at Pegu, which is 80 kilometers north of Rangoon.

Tin Maung Maung Than

98: A view of the northern section of the main platform of the Shwedagon Pagoda in Rangoon.
Tin Maung Maung Than

99: To the Buddhists, releasing captive sparrows is a merit-making act. Devotees buying the sparrows are at the foot of the Shwedagon Pagoda.
Tin Maung Maung Than

99

100-101: A Skaw Karen wedding near Chiangmai, north Thailand. The bridegroom, in a white shirt, and his party offer prayers to the tutelary spirit of the bride's village domain (100) and then exchange drinks with the village elders. The reception finishes with a village elder (101, man at right) and the ritual specialist from the bridegroom's village (101, man at left) pouring water over each other from a bamboo container. Water and the "state of cooling" is regarded as auspicious — for the bridal couple as well as for rice growing. The cymbals worn by the village elder are among the instruments providing music throughout the journey to the bride's village and the reception.

Ananda Rajah

102: Lionese priestesses in central Flores inside the ritual house attending to the most important annual ceremony preceeding rice sowing: they are opening sacred containers for rice.
Eriko Aoki

103: Buffalo horns are important lineage heirlooms to the Nage people of central Flores. They are kept in cult houses, together with the *sa'o waja*, the two wooden figures behind the horns. Traditionally, the *sa'o waja* were placed in front of the cult houses but are now kept indoors because many have been stolen.
Gregory Forth

102

103

104

104-105: *Thaipusam* is a major Hindu festival. In Singapore, devotees express their joy in the Serangoon Road area, which has a strong Indian community. Dressed in their finest garments, women wait for the religious procession (104) and help out at the stalls (105) which line the procession route and offer free drinks to everyone attending the festival. These gaily decorated stalls are financed by devotees.
Sharon Siddique and Nirmala Puru Shotam

105

REJOICING

106

107

106: Traditional Minangkabau weddings in Sumatra are elaborate. Brides wear full costumes and finely worked filigree head-dresses called *sunting*.
Cecilia Ng

107: The bride and bridegroom sit in state for the *bainai* ceremony when their fingers and palms are stained with henna.
Cecilia Ng

108: The bridal couple with their respective mothers.
Cecilia Ng

108

109: A bridal couple with their guests in the Laos village of Ban
Na Khoun Noi in 1963.
Ivan Polunin

110: A Skaw Karen bridegroom on one of three separate formal visits to the bride's home in a village near Chiangmai, north Thailand. He wears a modern white shirt over traditional garments.
Ananda Rajah

111: Musicians accompany a Skaw Karen wedding party.
Ananda Rajah

110

112

112-113: Unmarried Skaw Karen girls in north Thailand in a happy mood as they embroider blouses with decorated designs worn only by married women. They are preparing a wedding trousseau for the day when they will eventually marry.
Ananda Rajah

113

COOKING AND EATING

114

114-115: The Karen (of whom the Skaw
Karen are a sub-group) live in north
Thailand. A young Karen woman
winnows rice inside her house while an
old woman cooks at the hearth.
Suvit Rungvisai

115

116: Skaw Karen grandfather and grandson prepare glutinous rice cakes to be exchanged with other households in their village during the harvest celebrations.
Ananda Rajah

117

117-119: In central Flores,
an Endenese woman brings
coconut milk to the boil to
extract the oil. In another
household, women husk and
winnow rice to prepare food
for a funeral.
Eriko Aoki

119

120

121

120-121: At a Minangkabau wedding, the bridegroom's mother
and her matrilineal kin are ceremonially welcomed at the
bride's home (120) on the night of the *banai*. An array of food
prepared by the bride's lineage members (121) will be offered to
the bridegroom on his first overnight stay at the bride's home.
Cecilia Ng

124

122–124: A beansprout-grower soaking the beans (122 and 123) and examining the sprouts (124) in Singapore.
Henry Wong and Michael Neo

125

125: Workers of a Chinese herbal tea and medicine shop in Singapore share a meal provided by the proprietor.
Henry Wong and Michael Neo

126: Members of the clan in a village in central Flores, taking a ritual meal after an *étu* ceremony (see 177–179), an annual event held in major villages of the Nage people.
Gregory Forth

126

127: A Karen bride-to-be in north Thailand brews liquor for her wedding feast.
Suvit Rungvisai

127

PLANTING AND HARVESTING

128: A Batak family ploughing the field for rice planting on Samosir Island, Lake Toba, in Sumatra.
Fiona Clare

129-130: Rice harvesting by the Nage people in central Flores.
Gregory Forth

131: A Lionese man in central Flores threshing padi with his children "helping".
Eriko Aoki

132-134: Skaw Karen people harvesting hill rice in north Thailand.
Ananda Rajah

135: A Skaw Karen girl threshing rice.
Ananda Rajah

BUYING AND SELLING

136: Lanterns for sale during the Mid-Autumn
Festival in Singapore when children carry the lanterns
lighted with candles.
Henry Wong and Michael Neo

137

138

137–139: Singapore's garland-makers string jasmine blossoms with other flowers for sale in the Serangoon Road area which is predominantly Indian. Different kinds of garlands are used, for instance, for honouring deities, for adorning brides and bridegrooms and for decorating women's hairstyles.
Henry Wong and Michael Neo

139

140-141: Lionese pot-makers in central Flores bring their ware to a neighbouring Endenese village to trade for rice.
Eriko Aoki

141

TRAVELLING AND RESTING

142: Indonesian traders resting in their boats in Singapore in the early 1950s.
Ivan Polunin

142

143

144, 145: Resting on the veranda in south Thailand.
Institute for Southern Thai Studies

144: An old woman in her bed in a village in Krabi District, south Thailand.
Institute for Southern Thai Studies

144

145

Carriers or sledges can be drawn by buffaloes and used for carrying heavy loads like rice.

146, 148: Carriers in Surat Thani, south Thailand.
Institute for Southern Thai Studies

147: Murut carrier drawn by a buffalo, in Keningau, Sabah.
Ivan Polunin

147

146

148

149-150: Skaw Karen women moving through swidden fields collecting chillis in north Thailand.
Ananda Rajah

151: A Skaw Karen woman going home to her village in north Thailand after working in the field.
Ananda Rajah

152: A bamboo walkway at a
Bidayuh village in Sarawak.
Victor King

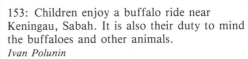

153: Children enjoy a buffalo ride near Keningau, Sabah. It is also their duty to mind the buffaloes and other animals.
Ivan Polunin

154: Skaw Karen children in north Thailand.
Ananda Rajah

155: A Malay villager having a good sit down inside an old dugout canoe in Johor, Malaysia.
Ivan Polunin

156-157: Murut carriers in Sabah walking through an area with newly planted hill padi. They pause for hourly rests. The baskets they carry are made by the Tambunan Dusun people.
Ivan Polunin

158: A pack of hunting dogs in a Murut house in Katubong, Sabah.
Ivan Polunin

159: An Endenese mother in central Flores with her children.
Eriko Aoki

161

160: A family in Siberut in traditional garments inside their home.
Wilfried Wagner

161-162: Walking and dugout cannoes are common means of travelling for the people of Siberut, Mentawai Islands, off the west coast of Sumatra.
Wilfried Wagner

162

163: A Skaw Karen man resting in between cutting cogon grass (*Imperata cylindrica*) which is used for thatching roofs in north Thailand.
Ananda Rajah

WORKING
AND PLAYING

164

166

164-166: Skaw Karen girls in north Thailand roll yarn into balls for weaving. The yarns are purchased from shops in northern Thai villages.
Ananda Rajah

167

167-168: Small scale manufacturers survive and some even thrive in unobtrusive corners of Singapore's urban landscape. Black vinegar is made according to secret family recipes (167). Barrels are still made by coopers (168) with teak imported from Thailand.
Henry Wong and Michael Neo

169

168

169: Spice grinding in Singapore's Serangoon Road area.
Sharon Siddique and Nirmala Puru Shotam

170

172

171

170–173: Singapore still has room for specialists who work with their hands. A scroll-maker brushes a piece of calligraphy to smooth out the paste (170). A cobbler makes *capals* or leather slippers (171). A goldsmith with his tools uses a skill which is traditionally passed on in the family (172). A frame-maker measures glass for framing Quranic inscriptions (173).
Henry Wong and Michael Neo

173

174: Lionese children in central Flores enjoy catching river shrimps.
Eriko Aoki

175: Bathing place at Rumah Chang, Sarawak.
Victor King

176: Children playing on the walkway of Kukup, a Chinese water village in Johor, Malaysia.
Ong Choo Suat

175

174

176

177–179: Hand to hand combat during the *étu* ceremony (see 126) is a test of strength between young men of the sponsoring village and those of other villages in the Nage region of central Flores.
Gregory Forth

178

177

179

180

180: A young Murut girl in Sabah, dressed up for the photograph.
Ivan Polunin

181

183-184: A Bidayuh woman cuts and trims bamboo for making rattan baskets in Sarawak.
Victor King

183

185

182

181-182: A Murut drinking party in Sabah features gong music as an added gaiety. Water is poured into jars of fermented mash and guests drink the alcoholic liquid through bamboo tubes. The jars are valuable antiques.
Ivan Polunin

184

185: A drummer in a Malay orchestra in Singapore in 1959.
Ivan Polunin

DECORATING

186

187

188

189

190

186–190: The fishing boats of Kelantan, Malaysia, are decorated in fine detail. Parts given special attention include the hull (190) and the headrest for the mast, carved in shapes of birds (189) and mythological beasts (186 and 187). These photographs were taken in 1977

Askandar Unglehrt

191

192

193

191: A Nage couple in central Flores wear their traditional garments and ornaments.
Gregory Forth

192: The design on this school wall in Niah, Sarawak, features a human figure. Traditionally, the design is reserved for the walls of funeral huts of aristocrats among the Kenyah people.
Victor King

193: Putting the finishing touches to a dragon head in Singapore. Working only part-time, the Chinese craftsman takes three and a half months to complete one dragon.
Henry Wong and Michael Neo

HEALING

194: A woman in Siberut, Mentawai Islands, prepares medicinal roots.
Wilfried Wagner

195: A physician trained in traditional Chinese medicine diagnoses an ailment for a customer as part of the services provided by a herbal tea and medicine shop in Singapore. The prescription is brewed on the spot for customers (see opposite page).
Henry Wong and Michael Neo

195

196-198: A traditional Chinese herbal tea and medicine shop in Singapore where roots and other items are sliced (196), weighed (197) and brewed in pots (198). Each preparation has its own special pot which is labelled.
Henry Wong and Michael Neo

196

197

198

REMEMBERING

199

199: In Riau, Indonesia, devout Muslims remember their departed. The grave within the enclosure is that of Raja Ali al-Haj, author of the *Tuhfat al-Nafis* and other Malay literary works. The cloth covering his grave markers indicates that prayers have been said for him.
Carl Trocki

200: Relatives pray at the graves of their loved ones periodically, particularly to mark special occasions. In the case of this Riau family, weekly prayers are held.
Vivienne Wee

200

201

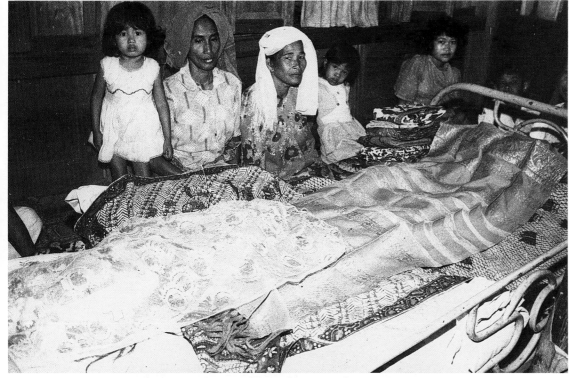

202

201–203: Among the Minangkabau in Sumatra, honouring the recently departed stretches over several days of mourning and ceremonial observances.

Relatives pay their respects to the deceased who has been covered with batik and other fine textiles. On the third day after the death, the matrilineal kin of the deceased observed a ceremony outside their house. Affines of the matrilineage of the deceased offer them *beras* or uncooked hulled rice. This ceremony marks the lifting of certain restrictions imposed on the matrilineage of the deceased. Restrictions include the non-attendance of weddings and not weaving.

Cecilia Ng

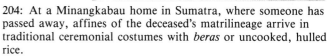

204

203

204: At a Minangkabau home in Sumatra, where someone has passed away, affines of the deceased's matrilineage arrive in traditional ceremonial costumes with *beras* or uncooked, hulled rice.

Cecilia Ng

Acknowledgements

Eriko Aoki

Asian Cultural Council

Fiona Clare

Wolfgang Clauss

Robert B. Cribb

Jacques Dournes

Gregory L. Forth

David E. Hughes

Institute for Southern Thai
Studies

Khoo Joo Ee

Victor T. King

Lim Chong Keat

Francisco Mañosa

Michael Neo

Cecilia Ng Siew Hua

Preecha Noonsuk

Ong Choo Suat

Ivan Polunin

Ananda Rajah

Nirmala Puru Shotam

Sharon Siddique

Southeast Asian Cultural
Research Programme

Margaret Sullivan

Sumet Jumsai

Suvit Rungvisai

Tin Maung Maung Than

Carl A. Trocki

Askandar Unglehrt

Wilfried Wagner

James F. Warren

Vivienne Wee

Henry Wong